Contents

- Introduction
- Chapter 1: Understanding Your Current Financial Situation
- Chapter 2: Creating a Budget
- Chapter 3: Managing Debt
- Chapter 4: Building an Emergency Fund
- Chapter 5: Investing Basics
- Chapter 6: Retirement Planning
- Chapter 7: Saving for Other Financial Goals
- Chapter 8: Protecting Your Financial Future
- Chapter 9: Increasing Income
- Chapter 10: Maintaining Financial Well-Being
- Conclusion

"Investing in yourself is the best investment you will ever make.
It will not only improve your life,
it will improve the lives of all those around you."

- Robin Sharma -

- Introduction -

Defining financial well-being

Financial well-being is a multidimensional concept that encompasses various aspects of an individual's financial health, security, and satisfaction. It goes beyond the mere accumulation of wealth and includes factors such as financial security, financial freedom, and financial resilience. Here is a detailed breakdown of the components that contribute to financial well-being:

Financial Security: Financial security refers to the ability to cover essential expenses and cope with unexpected financial shocks without significantly impacting one's standard of living. It involves having an adequate emergency fund, insurance coverage, and stable income sources to meet basic needs such as housing, food, healthcare, and transportation.

Financial Freedom: Financial freedom is the ability to make choices and pursue opportunities without being constrained by financial limitations. It involves having sufficient resources and flexibility to pursue personal goals, passions, and lifestyle preferences, whether it's traveling, starting a business, or retiring early. Achieving financial freedom often requires building passive income streams, reducing debt, and making prudent financial decisions.

Financial Stability: Financial stability refers to the ability to maintain a consistent financial situation over time, without experiencing significant fluctuations or hardships. It involves having a balanced financial life, with manageable levels of debt, stable income, and a sustainable budget that aligns with one's long-term financial goals. Financial stability provides a sense of predictability and peace of mind, reducing stress and anxiety related to financial matters.

Financial Resilience: Financial resilience is the capacity to bounce back from financial setbacks and adapt to changing circumstances effectively.

- Introduction -

It involves having a robust financial plan, adequate risk management strategies, and the ability to withstand economic downturns, job losses, or unexpected expenses without suffering long-term financial consequences. Building financial resilience requires having a diversified income, savings, and investment portfolio, as well as developing strong financial skills and knowledge.

Financial Well-being: Financial well-being is the overall state of satisfaction, confidence, and happiness individuals experience regarding their financial situation. It encompasses both objective financial indicators, such as income and net worth, as well as subjective factors, such as financial attitudes, behaviors, and perceptions. Financial well-being is influenced by various factors, including financial literacy, financial habits, financial goals, and the alignment between financial values and priorities.

In summary, financial well-being is a holistic concept that reflects individuals' ability to meet their financial needs, achieve their financial goals, and experience financial security, freedom, stability, and resilience. It involves managing financial resources effectively, making informed financial decisions, and cultivating healthy financial attitudes and behaviors that promote long-term financial health and happiness.

The importance of financial health

Financial health is crucial for individuals, families, businesses, and even entire economies. There are several key reasons why financial health is important:

- **Stability and Security:** Financial health provides stability and security by ensuring individuals and families can meet their basic needs and withstand unexpected financial shocks such as job loss and medical emergencies. Having sufficient savings, insurance coverage, and emergency funds safeguards against financial crises and reduces stress and anxiety.

- Introduction -

- **Goal Achievement:** Financial health enables individuals to pursue their goals and aspirations, whether it's buying a home, starting a business, traveling the world, or saving for retirement. By managing finances effectively and setting clear financial goals, individuals can make progress towards their dreams and live a fulfilling life.

- **Reduced Stress:** Financial stress is a significant source of anxiety and can negatively impact mental and physical health. Achieving financial health alleviates stress by providing a sense of control, predictability, and peace of mind. When individuals have a solid financial foundation, they can focus on other aspects of their lives without constantly worrying about money.

- **Improved Relationships:** Financial issues are a leading cause of relationship conflicts and breakdowns. Couples who are financially healthy tend to have stronger, more stable relationships because they can communicate openly about money, make joint financial decisions, and work together towards shared goals. Financial health fosters harmony and trust in personal and professional relationships.

- **Opportunity and Freedom:** Financial health opens up opportunities and gives individuals the freedom to make choices based on their values and priorities rather than financial constraints. Whether it's pursuing higher education, changing careers, or exploring new hobbies, financial health provides the flexibility and resources to seize opportunities and live life on one's own terms.

- **Retirement Preparedness:** Building financial health is essential for retirement preparedness. By saving and investing consistently throughout one's working years, individuals can build a retirement nest egg that provides financial security and independence in retirement. Planning for retirement early and maintaining financial health ensures a comfortable and fulfilling retirement lifestyle.

- Introduction -

- **Economic Growth:** On a broader scale, the financial health of individuals and households contributes to overall economic stability and growth. Healthy consumer spending, responsible borrowing and lending practices, and robust investment activity drive economic prosperity and create opportunities for job creation, innovation, and wealth creation.

Financial health is essential for individuals, families, communities, and economies to thrive. By prioritizing financial well-being, individuals can achieve stability, security, and success in all areas of life, leading to greater happiness, fulfillment, and prosperity.

What we will cover in this guide

1. Understanding Your Current Financial Situation
2. Creating a Budget
3. Managing Debt
4. Building an Emergency Fund
5. Investing Basics
6. Retirement Planning
7. Saving for Other Financial Goals
8. Protecting Your Financial Future
9. Increasing Income
10. Maintaining Financial Well-Being

Chapter 1:
Understanding Your Current Financial Situation

Assessing income sources

Assessing income sources is a crucial step in understanding one's financial situation and planning for financial well-being. Here are some key considerations when assessing income sources:

1. **Primary Income:** Primary income refers to the main source of income that individuals rely on to cover their regular expenses and financial obligations. This typically includes salaries or wages from employment, as well as any additional income earned from self-employment or freelance work.

2. **Secondary Income:** Secondary income consists of any additional sources of income beyond primary employment. This may include income from rental properties, investment dividends, royalties, side businesses, or part-time jobs. Secondary income streams can provide supplemental income and increase overall financial stability.

3. **Passive Income:** Passive income is income generated with minimal ongoing effort or active involvement. Examples of passive income sources include rental income, royalties from intellectual property, dividends from investments, interest from savings accounts or bonds, and affiliate marketing earnings. Passive income streams can provide a steady source of income without requiring constant time or effort.

4. **Investment Income:** Investment income refers to income generated from various types of investments, such as stocks, bonds, mutual funds, real estate, or retirement accounts. This income may come in the form of dividends, interest payments, capital gains, or distributions from investment vehicles. Assessing investment income helps individuals understand the returns they are earning on their investments and plan for future investment strategies.

5. **Retirement Income:** Retirement income includes any income received during retirement years from pension plans, retirement accounts (e.g., 401(k), IRA), Social Security benefits, annuities, or other retirement savings vehicles. Evaluating retirement income sources helps individuals determine if they are on track to meet their retirement goals and whether adjustments need to be made to retirement savings and investment plans.

6. **Non-Traditional Income:** Non-traditional income sources encompass any income streams that do not fit into conventional employment or investment categories. This may include income from gig economy jobs, freelance work, online businesses, or other non-traditional work arrangements. Assessing non-traditional income sources allows individuals to capitalize on emerging opportunities in the modern economy and diversify their income streams.

7. **Assessing Stability and Growth Potential:** When evaluating income sources, it's essential to consider the stability and growth potential of each source. Stable income sources provide consistent and predictable earnings, while income sources with growth potential offer the opportunity for increasing earnings over time. Diversifying income sources across stable and growth-oriented streams can enhance overall financial resilience and long-term wealth-building potential.

Assessing income sources involves examining the various sources of income available to individuals, understanding their characteristics, stability, and growth potential, and strategically leveraging them to achieve financial goals and objectives. By diversifying income streams and maximizing earning potential, individuals can enhance their financial well-being and create a more secure financial future.

- Chapter 1: Understanding Your Current Financial Situation -

Tracking expenses

Tracking expenses begins with categorizing your spending into different categories such as housing, transportation, groceries, utilities, entertainment, and debt payments. This categorization helps you understand where your money is going and identify areas where you may be overspending.

Keep track of all your expenses by recording each transaction, whether it's a cash purchase, credit card payment, or electronic transfer. You can use various tools such as budgeting apps, spreadsheets, or pen and paper to record your expenses regularly.

Review your spending patterns periodically to identify trends and areas where you can make adjustments. Look for recurring expenses that may be unnecessary or opportunities to cut back on discretionary spending.

Creating a budget based on your income and expenses allows you to allocate funds towards essential needs, savings goals, debt repayment, and discretionary spending categories. A well-planned budget helps you prioritize spending and ensures that you're living within your means.

Tracking expenses is an ongoing process, and it's essential to adjust your spending habits as needed to align with your financial goals and priorities. Regularly reviewing your budget and making adjustments helps you stay on track and make progress towards achieving financial well-being.

Overall, assessing income sources and tracking expenses are foundational practices in effective financial management. By understanding your income sources, maximizing earnings, and monitoring spending habits, you can build a solid financial foundation, achieve your goals, and secure your financial future.

Calculating net worth

Calculating net worth is a fundamental aspect of personal financial management that provides insight into an individual's overall financial health and stability. Net worth is determined by subtracting an individual's liabilities from their assets. Here's a step-by-step explanation of how to calculate net worth:

1. Identify your assets
- Assets are anything of value that an individual owns. This includes cash, savings, investments, retirement accounts, real estate properties, vehicles, valuable possessions such as jewelry or artwork, and any other assets with monetary value.

- Make a comprehensive list of all assets, including their estimated values. Be sure to include both liquid assets (those that can be easily converted to cash) and non-liquid assets (those that may take time to sell or convert to cash).

2. Calculate your total assets
- Once you have listed all assets and their respective values, add them together to determine the total value of your assets.

3. Identify your liabilities
- Liabilities are debts or financial obligations that an individual owes to others. This includes mortgages, car loans, student loans, credit card balances, personal loans, medical bills, and any other outstanding debts.

- Make a list of all liabilities, including the outstanding balances or amounts owed for each debt.

4. Calculate your total liabilities
- Add together the balances of all liabilities to determine the total amount of debt or financial obligations.

5. Subtract your liabilities from your assets
- To calculate net worth, subtract the total liabilities from the total assets. The formula for calculating net worth is:

- *Net Worth = Total Assets - Total Liabilities*

6. Interpret the Result
- If the result is a positive number, it means that the individual's assets exceed their liabilities, indicating a positive net worth.
- If the result is zero or close to zero, it means that the individual's assets are roughly equal to their liabilities.
- If the result is negative, it means that the individual's liabilities exceed their assets, indicating a negative net worth.

7. Review and update your net worth regularly
- It's important to review and update your net worth calculation regularly, such as annually or bi-annually, to track changes in your financial situation over time.

- Monitoring changes in net worth can help you assess progress toward financial goals, identify areas for improvement, and make informed decisions about budgeting, saving, investing, and debt management.

By calculating net worth regularly, individuals can gain a better understanding of their overall financial position, track financial progress, and make informed decisions to achieve long-term financial stability and security.

Identifying financial goals

Identifying financial goals is an essential step in personal financial planning, as it provides direction and purpose for managing money effectively. By identifying clear and meaningful financial goals, individuals can create a roadmap for their financial journey, make informed decisions, and take proactive steps to achieve greater financial security, stability, and success. Regularly review and update your goals as your circumstances and priorities evolve over time. Here's how to identify financial goals:

Reflect on your values and priorities
Start by reflecting on your values, aspirations, and priorities in life. Consider what matters most to you, both in the short term and the long term. Think about your personal, professional, and lifestyle goals, as well as your values related to family, health, education, career, leisure, and giving back to society.

Establish short-term and long-term goals
Differentiate between short-term goals (those you want to achieve within the next few months to a few years) and long-term goals (those you want to achieve over the next several years to decades). Short-term goals might include paying off credit card debt, saving for a vacation, or buying a new car. Long-term goals might include buying a home, saving for retirement, or funding your children's education.

Prioritize your goals
Rank your financial goals in order of importance or urgency. Consider which goals are most critical to your overall well-being and which can be postponed or adjusted if necessary.

Focus on addressing high-priority goals first, while also allocating resources toward achieving medium- and low-priority goals over time.

Make your goals specific, Measurable, Achievable, Relevant, and Time-Bound (S.M.A.R.T.)

Ensure that your financial goals are SMART:

- **Specific:** Clearly define what you want to accomplish.
- **Measurable:** Determine how you will measure progress and success.
- **Achievable:** Set goals that are realistic and attainable based on your current financial situation and resources.
- **Relevant:** Align your goals with your values, priorities, and life circumstances.
- **Time-Bound:** Establish a timeline for achieving each goal, setting deadlines and milestones along the way.

Consider creating different categories of financial goals

Financial goals can be categorized into various areas, including:

- **Saving and Investing:** Building an emergency fund, saving for retirement, investing in the stock market, or funding specific financial milestones.
- **Debt Management:** Paying off high-interest debt, such as credit card balances or student loans, to reduce financial stress and improve cash flow.
- **Lifestyle and Enjoyment:** Budgeting for leisure activities, travel, hobbies, and other experiences that bring joy and fulfillment.
- **Career and Education:** Investing in professional development, furthering your education, or pursuing career advancement opportunities.
- **Family and Relationships:** Supporting family members financially, planning for children's education, or contributing to charitable causes.

Write down your goals and create an action plan

Once you've identified your financial goals, write them down clearly and concisely. Use the SMART criteria to refine and articulate each goal effectively.

Develop an action plan outlining specific steps, strategies, and timelines for achieving each goal. Break down larger goals into smaller, manageable tasks to make progress more attainable.

Chapter 2:
Creating a Budget

The importance of budgeting

Budgeting is one of the most crucial aspects of personal financial management. It is essential for achieving financial success and well-being. If done properly, it provides individuals with the tools and framework to manage their money effectively, control expenses, achieve financial goals, and build a solid foundation for long-term financial security and prosperity.

A budget allows individuals to track their income and expenses, providing a clear picture of their financial situation. It helps them understand where their money is coming from, where it's going, and how it's being used.

By creating a budget, individuals can identify unnecessary or frivolous expenses and make informed spending decisions. Budgeting helps prioritize essential expenses while cutting back on non-essential ones, thereby reducing overspending and increasing savings.

Setting up a budget enables individuals to allocate funds toward specific financial goals, such as building an emergency fund, paying off debt, saving for a home, or investing for retirement. By setting aside money for these goals within the budget, individuals can make steady progress toward achieving them.

It also helps individuals manage debt more effectively by allocating funds toward debt repayment. By including debt payments as part of the budget, individuals can create a structured plan for paying off debt faster and reducing interest costs over time.

Proper budgeting allows individuals to set aside funds for unexpected expenses or emergencies, such as medical bills, car repairs, or job loss.

By building an emergency fund within the budget, individuals can mitigate the financial impact of unexpected events and avoid going into debt to cover unforeseen costs.

Overall, improved budgeting promotes financial discipline, responsibility, and accountability. It helps individuals develop healthy financial habits, such as living within their means, saving regularly, and planning for the future. By adhering to a budget, individuals can improve their financial health, reduce financial stress, and achieve greater financial stability and security.

Different budgeting methods

There are various budgeting methods that individuals can use to manage their finances effectively. The most suitable method depends on personal preferences, financial goals, lifestyle, and individual circumstances. Here are some common budgeting methods:

Zero-Based Budgeting
Zero-based budgeting requires allocating every dollar of income to specific categories, ensuring that income minus expenses equal zero.

With this method, individuals assign all their income to various expense categories, including fixed expenses (e.g., rent, utilities), variable expenses (e.g., groceries, entertainment), savings, and debt repayment.

By giving every dollar a purpose, zero-based budgeting helps individuals prioritize spending, eliminate wasteful expenses, and maximize savings and debt repayment.

50/30/20 Rule (or the Balanced Money Formula)
The Balanced Money Formula provides a simple guideline for balancing spending between necessities, wants, and financial goals, helping individuals achieve financial stability and flexibility.

This 50/30/20 rule divides your net income into three categories:
- **50% for needs:** This includes essential expenses such as housing, utilities, groceries, transportation, and insurance.
- **30% for wants:** This category covers discretionary expenses such as dining out, entertainment, travel, and non-essential purchases.
- **20% for savings and debt repayment:** This portion is allocated toward savings goals (e.g., emergency fund, retirement savings) and debt repayment (e.g., credit card debt, student loans).

The Envelope System

An envelope system involves allocating cash into envelopes labeled with different spending categories, such as groceries, entertainment, dining out, and transportation.

Individuals withdraw cash from their bank account and distribute it into the appropriate envelopes based on their budgeted amounts for each category.

Throughout the month, individuals can only spend from the designated envelopes, providing a tangible and visual way to track spending and avoid overspending in specific areas.

Pay Yourself First

The pay-yourself-first method involves prioritizing savings by automatically setting aside a portion of income for savings and investments before allocating funds to other expenses.

Individuals can set up automatic transfers from their checking account to savings or investment accounts, treating savings as a non-negotiable expense.

By paying themselves first, individuals ensure that they prioritize their financial goals and build savings consistently over time.

Percentage-Based Budgeting

A percentage-based budgeting system involves allocating a fixed percentage of income to different expense categories based on pre-defined guidelines.

Common percentages may include housing (25-35% of income), transportation (10-15%), food (10-15%), debt repayment (5-10%), savings (10-15%), and discretionary spending (5-10%).

This method provides a flexible framework for budgeting based on income levels and individual financial priorities.

Reverse Budgeting

This involves setting savings goals first, before allocating the remaining income toward expenses.

Individuals determine their desired savings targets for various financial goals, such as emergency funds, retirement savings, or major purchases.

After setting aside savings contributions, individuals use the remaining funds for living expenses and discretionary spending.

These are just a few examples of budgeting methods that individuals can use to manage their finances effectively. It's important to choose a budgeting method that aligns with your financial priorities and helps you achieve your long-term financial objectives.

Developing a personalised budget

Developing a personalized budget involves creating a plan that reflects your unique financial situation, goals, and priorities. By following these steps, you can take control of your finances, achieve your financial goals, and build a brighter financial future for yourself and your family.

Here's a step-by-step guide to help you develop a personalised budget:

Assess your financial situation
- Gather information about your income, expenses, assets, liabilities, and financial goals.
- Calculate your total monthly income, including salaries, wages, bonuses, side hustles, investment income, and any other sources of income.
- Determine your total monthly expenses, including fixed expenses (e.g., rent or mortgage, utilities, insurance) and variable expenses (e.g., groceries, transportation, entertainment).

Define your financial goals
- As previously explained, it is important to identify short-term, medium-term, and long-term financial goals. These may include paying off debt, saving for emergencies, buying a home, funding education, or planning for retirement.
- Set specific, measurable, achievable, relevant, and time-bound (**SMART**) goals to guide your budgeting process (Refer to Chapter 1).

Categorise your expenses
- Organise your expenses into categories such as housing, transportation, food, utilities, healthcare, debt payments, savings, investments, entertainment, and miscellaneous expenses.
- Review your past spending habits and adjust categories as needed to reflect your current lifestyle and priorities.

Allocate funds to each category
- Determine how much you want to allocate to each expense category based on your income and financial goals.
- Start with essential expenses such as housing, utilities, and groceries, and then allocate funds to other categories based on their priority and importance.
- Be realistic and flexible when allocating funds, and consider making adjustments to ensure your budget is achievable.

Use a budgeting method that works for you
- Choose a budgeting method that aligns with your preferences, lifestyle, and financial goals. *(These popular budgeting methods were explained in our previous sub-section called **Different budgeting methods**)*
- The best way to establish which budgeting style works best for you is by experimenting with the different budgeting methods until find one that suits your needs and helps you achieve your financial goals.

Monitor and adjust your budget
- Track your spending regularly to ensure you're sticking to your budget and making progress toward your financial goals.
- Review your budget periodically and make adjustments as needed based on changes in income, expenses, priorities, and financial circumstances.

It is important to realise that you may not necessarily achieve the perfect budget right off the bat, however, don't let this discourage you from trying again. Stay disciplined and committed to your budget, be flexible and willing to adapt to changes over time.

Top 10 tips to help you stick to your budget

Sticking to a budget can be challenging, and may take multiple attempts until you find a method that best suits your goals and lifestyle. With discipline, consistency, and some practical strategies, it's entirely achievable. Here are some expert tips to help you stay on track with your budget:

1. Always ensure your goals are achievable
Make sure you set specific financial goals that motivate you and align with your values and priorities. Having clear objectives will help you stay focused and committed to your budget.

2. Monitor your spending regularly

Make use of budgeting apps, spreadsheets, or even pen and paper to track your expenses and identify areas where you may be overspending. This will ensure you stay within your set budget limits.

3. Visualise your spending

Allocating cash to different spending categories using the cash envelope system is one of the best methods to follow if you are a visual planner. This tangible approach can help you to only spend what's available in each envelope and subsequently prevent overspending.

4. Automate your savings and payments

Set up automatic transfers to savings accounts and debit order payments to ensure you're consistently saving and paying your bills on time. Automation removes the temptation to spend money earmarked for savings or bills within your budget outlay.

5. Practice delayed gratification

Before making non-essential purchases, give yourself time to assess whether an item is something you truly need or if it is simply something you want. Delaying gratification can help curb impulse spending and also prevent buyer's remorse in the future.

6. Use the 24-hour rule

Use the '24-hour rule' for significant purchases. Wait at least 24 hours before purchasing to identify if this is something you still want or need. This works hand in hand with the delayed gratification method as it gives you time to consider the purchase more thoughtfully to avoid impulse buys.

7. Plan your spending in advance

By creating a weekly or monthly spending plan in advance, it will allow you to allocate funds to different expense categories based on your budget and prioritize essential expenses over discretionary ones.

8. Teach yourself to practice mindful spending

Be mindful of your spending habits to help identify triggers that lead to impulse spending (for example, sales and special offers). When making purchasing decisions, it is important to get into the habit of asking yourself the following; *"Does this item align with my budget and financial goals?"*

9. Review your budget regularly and adjust accordingly

Try to look at your budget periodically to assess your progress, and identify areas of improvement, so you can make the necessary adjustments. Your life circumstances and financial priorities will change from time to time, and therefore your budget should always be flexible and adaptable.

10. Celebrate your milestones and progress

Don't be shy to celebrate your milestones and achievements - whether it's something big such as reaching a savings goal, paying off debt, or simply sticking to your budget over a certain period. Acknowledging your successes will help to keep you motivated and inspired to keep going.

By implementing these tips and staying committed to your budgeting goals, you can develop healthy financial habits, achieve your financial objectives, and ultimately build a stronger financial future.

Chapter 3:
Managing Debt

Identifying different types of debt

Whether you like it or not, in today's day and age, we all have some form of debt. By understanding and identifying the types of debt you have and their associated terms, interest rates, and repayment options, you can develop a strategy to pay off debt efficiently, minimise interest costs, and ultimately achieve financial freedom. Here are some common types of debt:

1. Consumer Debt
- Credit Card Debt: Debt accrued from using credit cards to make purchases or cover expenses. Credit card debt often carries high-interest rates, making it costly to maintain balances over time.
- Personal Loans: Unsecured loans obtained from banks, credit unions, or online lenders for various purposes, such as consolidating debt, funding emergencies, or covering personal expenses.
- Payday Loans: Short-term, high-interest loans typically taken out by individuals facing cash flow shortages between paychecks. Payday loans often come with exorbitant fees and can trap borrowers in cycles of debt.

2. Mortgage Debt
- Home Mortgage: Debt incurred to purchase a home or property. Mortgages are secured loans, with the property serving as collateral. They typically have lower interest rates compared to other types of consumer debt.
- Home Equity Loans: Loans that allow homeowners to borrow against the equity in their homes. Home equity loans can be used for various purposes, such as home improvements, debt consolidation, or major expenses.

3. Student Loans
- **Federal Student Loans**: Loans issued by the U.S. Department of Education to help students finance higher education. Federal student loans offer borrower protections and flexible repayment options.
- **Private Student Loans**: Loans obtained from private lenders, such as banks or credit unions, to cover educational expenses. Private student loans often have higher interest rates and fewer borrower protections than federal loans.

4. Vehicle Finance
- **Car Loans**: Loans used to finance the purchase of a vehicle. Car loans can be obtained from banks, credit unions, or auto dealerships and are secured by the vehicle itself. The terms and interest rates of car loans can vary based on factors such as credit history, loan amount, and repayment terms.

5. Medical Debt
- Debt incurred from medical expenses, including hospital bills, doctor's fees, prescription medications, and medical procedures. Medical debt can arise from unexpected medical emergencies or ongoing healthcare needs and may be covered by health insurance to varying degrees.

6. Business Debt
- Loans and credit facilities taken on by businesses to fund operations, expansion, or capital investments. Business debt can include lines of credit, business loans, equipment financing, or merchant cash advances.

Strategies to pay off your debt

Given the challenging global economic climate most of us have been facing over the past couple of years, it is safe to say that we can all relate to the stress and overwhelming feeling associated with debt repayments. However, with careful planning, determination, discipline, and effort, you can take control of your financial future and work towards becoming debt-free again. We have researched and identified some of the most successful strategies to help you pay off your debt effectively:

1. Budget, budget, budget!
- As discussed in Chapter 2, start by assessing your income, expenses, and debt obligations. Create a budget that allocates a portion of your income to debt repayments, your essential expenses, and savings goals.

2. Prioritise your debts
- Make a list of all your debts, including their balances, repayment periods, interest rates, and minimum monthly payments.
- From here, you can start prioritising your debts based on various factors such as interest rates, outstanding balances, and type of debt, etc.
- Consider using the debt avalanche method or the debt snowball method to accelerate your debt payoff progress. The debt avalanche method involves paying off debts with the highest interest rates first, while the debt snowball method lets you pay off debts with the smallest balances first.

3. Make extra payments wherever possible
- Try to allocate any extra funds, such as bonuses, tax refunds, or windfalls, toward debt repayment.
- Work towards increasing your monthly debt payments by cutting back on discretionary expenses or finding additional sources of income through side hustles or freelance work if possible.

4. Consider consolidating your debt
- Explore debt consolidation options, such as balance transfer credit cards or debt consolidation loans, to combine multiple debts into a single, more manageable payment with a lower interest rate.
- Be cautious when consolidating debt and ensure that you're not trading short-term savings for long-term financial strain.

5. Negotiate with your creditors
- Reach out to your creditors to negotiate lower interest rates, reduced fees, or more favorable repayment terms. Many people don't realise that most creditors are always willing to work with borrowers experiencing financial hardship and may offer hardship programs or payment plans to help them get back on track.

6. Create automatic payments (Debit orders)
- Set up automatic payments for your debts to ensure you never miss a payment and incur late fees or penalties.
- You can also consider opting for bi-weekly payments instead of monthly repayments to accelerate your debt payoff and reduce interest costs.

7. Try to stay motivated
- Paying off debt is never easy or pleasant. Celebrate small victories along the way, such as paying off a credit card or reaching a debt milestone to keep yourself motivated.
- Keep visual reminders of your progress, such as a debt payoff tracker or a vision board, to stay focused on your long-term goals.
- Don't underestimate the importance of your mental well-being during this process. Surround yourself with a supportive network of friends, family, or financial advisors who can offer encouragement and accountability.

8. Don't be afraid to seek professional help if needed
- Stress is always a big demotivating factor when it comes to debt repayments. If you're struggling to manage your debt or develop a repayment plan, consider seeking assistance from a certified credit counselor or financial advisor.
- These professionals can provide personalized advice, debt management strategies, and resources to help you navigate your financial challenges and achieve relief from debt.

Remember that paying off debt takes time, discipline, and perseverance. Stay committed to your debt repayment plan and always stay focused on your goals,

How to avoid and manage debt traps

Avoiding and managing debt traps is essential for maintaining financial stability and avoiding long-term financial struggles. By implementing these strategies and staying vigilant about your finances, you can avoid falling into debt traps and build a solid foundation for long-term financial well-being.

1. Make sure you understand your finances
By assessing your current financial situation (including your income, expenses, assets, and debts) you will gain a better understanding of your spending habits, cash flow, and overall financial health. This is valuable knowledge to help you identify potential areas of improvement.

2. Build up an emergency fund
No one can foresee what will happen in the future, so it is crucial that you establish an emergency fund to cover unexpected expenses and financial emergencies, such as medical bills, car repairs, or job loss. Aim to save enough to cover three to six months' worth of living expenses in a high-yield savings account or other easily accessible account. (More about this in Chapter 4)

3. Live below your means

Practice frugality and avoid lifestyle inflation by living below your means and resisting the urge to overspend on non-essential items. Learn to differentiate between your needs and wants, and prioritize spending on necessities while limiting discretionary expenses.

4. Avoid high-interest debt

Always be cautious when taking on debt, especially high-interest debt such as payday loans, cash advances, or credit card debt. If possible, consider alternative financing options or explore other avenues to meet financial needs without resorting to high-cost borrowing.

5. Credit cards are not your friend

Use credit cards responsibly and avoid carrying high balances or maxing out your credit limits, as this may affect your credit profile negatively over time. Avoid falling into a debt cycle by paying your credit card balances in full each month, as this will avoid accumulating additional interest charges.

6. Seek Financial Education

Educate yourself about personal finance, debt management, and financial planning through books, online resources, workshops, or financial literacy programs. You can also take advantage of free resources and tools offered by reputable organisations, agencies, or nonprofit organizations. to help improve your financial literacy and sharpen your financial decision-making skills.

Chapter 4:
Building an Emergency Fund

The importance of an emergency fund

If COVID19 taught us anything, it's the importance of having an emergency fund. By prioritizing the establishment and maintenance of an emergency fund, individuals can better withstand financial challenges, avoid debt traps, and navigate life's uncertainties with greater confidence and security. There are are several great reasons that highlight the importance of having an emergency fund.

Financial security: An emergency fund provides financial security by ensuring individuals have funds readily available to cover unexpected expenses without resorting to high-interest debt or liquidating assets. It offers peace of mind knowing that you have a cushion to fall back on during challenging times.

A safety net against loss of income: In the event of a job loss, illness, or disability preventing you from working, an emergency fund can bridge the gap between income streams and cover essential expenses such as housing, utilities, groceries, and medical bills until you're able to get back on your feet.

Protection against unforeseen expenses: Life is unpredictable, and unforeseen expenses such as car repairs, home maintenance issues, medical emergencies, or sudden travel needs can arise at any time. Having an emergency fund allows you to handle these expenses without derailing your financial plans or accumulating high-interest debt.

It helps you avoid high-interest debt: Without an emergency fund, individuals may resort to borrowing money through credit cards, payday loans, or personal loans to cover unexpected expenses. These forms of debt often come with high interest rates, fees, and unfavorable terms, leading to a cycle of debt that can be difficult to escape.

Maintains financial stability: An emergency fund acts as a buffer against financial shocks, helping individuals maintain stability and continuity in their financial lives. It prevents minor setbacks from spiraling into major crises and allows individuals to stay on track with their long-term financial goals.

Helps reduce stress and anxiety: Financial stress is a significant source of anxiety for many people. Knowing that you have an emergency fund in place can alleviate worries about how to handle unexpected expenses or income disruptions, allowing you to focus on other aspects of your life with greater peace of mind.

Building an opportunity fund: In addition to covering emergencies, an emergency fund can also serve as an opportunity fund for pursuing personal or professional opportunities that arise unexpectedly. Whether it's taking advantage of a job opportunity, investing in a business venture, or pursuing further education, having liquid savings can provide the flexibility to seize opportunities as they arise.

How much to save in an emergency fund

Determining how much to save in an emergency fund depends on various factors, including your financial situation, expenses, income stability, and risk tolerance. While there isn't a one-size-fits-all answer, here are some guidelines to help you establish an appropriate emergency fund target:

Calculate your monthly expenses:
- Start by calculating your average monthly expenses, including essential costs such as housing, utilities, groceries, transportation, insurance, debt payments, and other necessary expenses.
- Consider both fixed expenses (e.g., rent/mortgage, insurance premiums) and variable expenses (e.g., groceries, dining out), as well as any irregular expenses (e.g., medical bills, car repairs).

Assess your income stability:
- Evaluate the stability of your income sources, including salaries, wages, bonuses, commissions, and any other sources of income.
- If you have a steady income, aim to save at least three to six months' worth of living expenses in your emergency fund.
- If you have variable income or work in an industry prone to volatility or layoffs, consider saving six to twelve months' worth of expenses or more to provide a larger safety net.

Consider all your financial obligations:
- Take into account any additional financial obligations or potential emergencies unique to your situation, such as healthcare costs, childcare expenses, or caring for aging parents.
- Factor in any debt repayments, such as student loans, credit card debt, or mortgage payments, and ensure your emergency fund can cover these obligations in case of income loss or unexpected expenses.

Assess your risk tolerance:
- Consider your risk tolerance and comfort level when determining the size of your emergency fund. If you prefer a larger safety net or have concerns about job security or economic uncertainty, err on the side of saving more.
- Conversely, if you have a stable income, robust insurance coverage, or access to other financial resources, you may be comfortable with a smaller emergency fund.

Set a target savings goal:
- Based on your monthly expenses, income stability, financial obligations, and risk tolerance, set a target savings goal for your emergency fund.
- Aim to save enough to cover your essential expenses for the desired timeframe (e.g., three to six months) or longer if you have higher risk factors or prefer a larger safety net.

Review and adjust your emergency fund regularly:
- Regularly review your emergency fund target and adjust it as needed based on changes in your financial situation, expenses, income, or risk factors.
- Reassess your emergency fund goal annually or after significant life events such as job changes, income fluctuations, or major expenses.

Ultimately, the amount you save in your emergency fund should provide a sufficient financial cushion to cover essential expenses and weather unforeseen circumstances without relying on high-interest debt or depleting other savings accounts. Always customise your emergency fund target based on your individual needs, circumstances, and financial goals.

Best places to keep your emergency fund savings

When it comes to storing your emergency fund savings, the key considerations are accessibility, safety, and potential for growth. Here are some of the best places to keep your emergency fund:

1. High-yield savings account:
- A high-yield savings account offers a combination of accessibility and higher interest rates compared to traditional savings accounts. They are FDIC-insured (or NCUA-insured for credit unions) up to the maximum allowed by law, typically $250,000 per depositor per institution.
- Look for online banks or credit unions that offer competitive interest rates with no monthly fees or minimum balance requirements. Consider factors such as ease of access, customer service, and account features when choosing a bank.

2. Money market account:
- Money market accounts (MMAs) are similar to savings accounts but may offer slightly higher interest rates and additional features such as check-writing privileges or debit cards.

- MMAs are also FDIC-insured or NCUA-insured, making them a safe option for storing emergency savings.

3. Certificates of deposit (CDs):
- Certificates of Deposit (CDs) offer higher interest rates than savings accounts or MMAs but require you to lock in your funds for a specified term, such as six months, one year, or longer.
- Consider building a CD ladder by staggering maturity dates to maintain liquidity while taking advantage of higher interest rates. Be mindful of early withdrawal penalties if you need to access funds before the CD matures.

4. Online bank checking account:
- Some online banks offer checking accounts with high interest rates and no monthly fees or minimum balance requirements. While less common, these accounts may offer better yields than traditional checking accounts.
- Look for checking accounts with features like ATM fee reimbursements, mobile banking, and easy transfers to linked savings accounts.

5. Cash reserve:
- Keeping a portion of your emergency fund in cash or a liquid account can provide immediate access to funds in case of emergencies or situations where electronic payments are not accepted.
- Consider maintaining a small cash reserve in a secure location at home or in a fireproof safe, along with easy-to-access liquid funds in a bank account.

6. Brokerage account (taxable investment account):
- While not as liquid as savings accounts or CDs, taxable brokerage accounts offer the potential for higher returns through investments in stocks, bonds, or mutual funds.
- Reserve brokerage accounts for emergency funds only after fully funding tax-advantaged retirement accounts and assessing your risk tolerance, as investments in the market can fluctuate in value and are not FDIC-insured.

When choosing where to keep your emergency fund, prioritize safety, liquidity, and growth potential based on your individual needs, preferences, and risk tolerance. Diversifying your emergency fund across multiple accounts or asset classes can provide a balance of accessibility, security, and potential returns while ensuring you're prepared for unexpected expenses or financial emergencies.

Top 10 tips for building an emergency fund

Building an emergency fund takes time, discipline, and commitment, but the financial security and peace of mind it provides are well worth the effort. Stay focused on your goals, stay disciplined with your savings habits, and be patient as you work toward building a solid financial foundation for yourself and your family. Here are the top tips to help you build and grow your emergency fund:

1. Set a savings goal:
Start by setting a specific savings goal for your emergency fund. Aim to save at least three to six months' worth of living expenses to cover essential costs in case of unexpected financial setbacks or emergencies.

2. Create a budget:
Develop a budget that outlines your income, expenses, and savings goals. Identify areas where you can cut back on discretionary spending and allocate those savings toward your emergency fund.

3. Automate your savings:
Set up automatic transfers from your checking account to your designated emergency fund account each month. Treat your emergency fund savings like a non-negotiable expense to ensure consistent contributions.

4. Start small and be consistent:
If saving a significant amount seems daunting, start small and gradually increase your savings over time. Even small, consistent contributions can add up over time and help you reach your savings goal.

5. Cut expenses as much as possible:
Look for opportunities to reduce your expenses and free up more money for savings. Consider cutting back on non-essential expenses such as dining out, entertainment, subscription services, or impulse purchases.

6. Boost your income:
Explore ways to increase your income, such as negotiating a raise or promotion at work, taking on a side hustle or freelance work, selling unused items, or renting out space in your home.

7. Save windfalls and bonuses:
Whenever you receive unexpected windfalls or bonuses, such as tax refunds, work bonuses, or cash gifts, resist the temptation to spend them frivolously. Instead, allocate these funds toward your emergency fund to accelerate your savings progress.

8. Use windfalls wisely:
 - If you receive unexpected or one-time financial windfalls, such as inheritance, lottery winnings, or a settlement, consider using a portion of the funds to bolster your emergency fund and secure your financial future.

9. Reduce your debt:
Prioritize paying off high-interest debt, such as credit card debt or payday loans, to free up more money for savings. Once you've paid off your debt, redirect the funds you were using for debt payments toward your emergency fund.

10. Stay motivated:
Keep your savings goals visible and stay motivated by tracking your progress regularly. Celebrate milestones along the way to keep yourself motivated and committed to building your emergency fund.

Chapter 5:
Investing Basics

Understanding your investment options

Investments are crucial for building wealth, achieving financial goals, and securing your financial future so it is important that you understand your investment options. These are some of the key investment options to consider:

1. Stocks:
Stocks represent ownership shares in publicly traded companies. Investing in stocks offers the potential for significant long-term growth but comes with higher volatility and risk. Stocks can be purchased individually or through mutual funds, exchange-traded funds (ETFs), or index funds, which offer diversification across multiple stocks.

2. Bonds:
Bonds are debt securities issued by governments, municipalities, corporations, or other entities. When you invest in bonds, you're essentially lending money to the issuer in exchange for regular interest payments and the return of the principal at maturity. Bonds are generally considered less risky than stocks but offer lower potential returns.

3. Mutual funds:
Mutual funds pool money from multiple investors to invest in a diversified portfolio of stocks, bonds, or other assets. They're managed by professional portfolio managers, who make investment decisions on behalf of investors. Mutual funds offer diversification, liquidity, and professional management but may come with fees and expenses.

4. Exchange-traded funds (ETFs):
ETFs are similar to mutual funds but trade on stock exchanges like individual stocks.

They offer diversified exposure to various asset classes, sectors, or regions and typically have lower expense ratios than mutual funds. ETFs can be bought and sold throughout the trading day at market prices.

5. Real estate:
Real estate investments involve purchasing properties (such as residential, commercial, or rental properties) with the expectation of generating rental income and/or capital appreciation. Real estate offers diversification and potential tax benefits but requires significant capital, maintenance, and management.

6. Retirement accounts:
Retirement accounts such as 401(k)s, IRAs (Traditional and Roth), and SEP-IRAs offer tax-advantaged ways to save for retirement. Contributions to these accounts may be tax-deductible (Traditional) or grow tax-free (Roth) until retirement age. Many employers offer matching contributions to 401(k) accounts, providing additional incentives to save for retirement.

7. Certificates of deposit (CDs) and savings accounts:
CDs and savings accounts are low-risk, interest-bearing accounts offered by banks and credit unions. CDs have fixed terms and interest rates, while savings accounts offer liquidity and easy access to funds. These options provide safety of principal but typically offer lower returns compared to other investments.

8. Alternative investments:
Alternative investments such as commodities, hedge funds, private equity, and cryptocurrencies offer alternative sources of returns and diversification but often come with higher risk, complexity, and liquidity constraints. They may be suitable for sophisticated investors with higher risk tolerance and longer investment horizons.

9. Robo-advisors:
Robo-advisors are automated investment platforms that use algorithms and computer algorithms to provide portfolio management services.

They offer low-cost, diversified investment portfolios based on your risk tolerance, financial goals, and time horizon.

10. Education savings accounts:
Education savings accounts such as 529 plans and Coverdell Education Savings Accounts (ESAs) help families save for future education expenses. Contributions to these accounts grow tax-deferred and can be withdrawn tax-free for qualified education expenses.

Before investing, it's essential to assess your risk tolerance, investment objectives, time horizon, and financial situation. Consider seeking guidance from a financial advisor or doing thorough research to make informed investment decisions aligned with your goals and risk tolerance. Diversification across multiple asset classes and periodic portfolio rebalancing can help manage risk and optimise long-term returns.

Risk tolerance assessment

Assessing your risk tolerance is a critical step when investing money, as it helps you determine the level of investment risk you are comfortable with and align your investment choices accordingly. This is how you can assess your risk tolerance when investing:

1. Understand your financial situation:
Start by evaluating your financial situation, including your income, expenses, savings, debt, and financial goals. Consider factors such as your age, employment status, dependents, and other financial obligations.

2. Define your investment goals:
Clarify your investment objectives, time horizon, and financial goals. Are you investing for retirement, education, a major purchase, or wealth accumulation? Determine when you'll need access to your invested funds and how long you plan to keep your investments.

3. Assess how comfortable you are with investment risks:

Evaluate your comfort level with investment risk by considering how you would react to fluctuations in the value of your investments. Ask yourself questions such as:

- How would you feel if your investment portfolio experienced a significant decline in value?
- Are you willing to accept short-term volatility in exchange for potentially higher long-term returns?
- How would you react if your investment portfolio underperformed relative to your expectations or financial goals?

4. Consider your investment horizon:

Your investment horizon, or the length of time you plan to hold your investments, can influence your risk tolerance. Generally, longer investment horizons allow for a higher tolerance for risk, as there is more time to recover from market downturns.

5. Evaluate your past investment experience:

Reflect on your past investment experience, if any, and how you reacted to different market conditions and investment outcomes. Consider any lessons learned from previous investment successes or failures.

6. Use risk tolerance assessments:

Many financial institutions and online investment platforms offer risk tolerance assessments or questionnaires to help investors determine their risk tolerance. These assessments typically ask about your financial situation, investment goals, time horizon, and attitudes toward risk.

7. Consult with a financial advisor:

Consider seeking advice from a qualified financial advisor or investment professional who can help assess your risk tolerance and develop an appropriate investment strategy tailored to your financial goals and risk preferences.

8. Diversification and asset allocation:
Based on your risk tolerance, diversify your investment portfolio across different asset classes, such as stocks, bonds, cash equivalents, and alternative investments, to manage risk and maximise potential returns.
Adjust your asset allocation based on your risk tolerance, investment objectives, and changing market conditions over time.

9. Regularly review and reassess:
Periodically review your investment portfolio and reassess your risk tolerance, especially during major life events, changes in financial circumstances, or shifts in market conditions. Adjust your investment strategy as needed to stay aligned with your risk tolerance and investment goals.

By carefully assessing your risk tolerance and aligning your investment choices with your financial goals and comfort level with risk, you can build a diversified investment portfolio that meets your needs and helps you achieve long-term financial success.

Setting investment goals

By setting clear, achievable, and measurable investment goals, you can create a roadmap for success and make informed decisions to build wealth, achieve financial security, and realize your long-term financial aspirations. Follow this step-by-step guide to setting investment goals:

1. Establish clear financial objectives for yourself:
Start by clarifying your financial objectives and what you hope to achieve through investing. Your goals may include retirement planning, funding education expenses, buying a home, starting a business, or achieving financial independence.

2. Quantify your goals:
Specify the amount of money you need to achieve each financial goal.

Break down your goals into short-term (less than three years), medium-term (three to ten years), and long-term (more than ten years) objectives.

3. Establish a realistic timeframe:
Determine the time in which you aim to achieve each investment goal. Your time horizon will influence your investment strategy and asset allocation decisions.

4. Consider your risk tolerance:
As discussed in our previous section (risk tolerance assessment) it is always important to assess your risk tolerance and comfort level with investment risk. Your risk tolerance will influence the types of investments you choose and the level of volatility you can tolerate in your investment portfolio.

5. Always be realistic and specific:
Set realistic and specific investment goals that are achievable within your financial means. Avoid setting overly ambitious or vague goals that may be difficult to attain.

6. Prioritise your goals:
Your investment goals should needs to be prioritised based on their importance and urgency. It is best to focus on funding essential goals such as retirement and education savings before pursuing discretionary goals.

7. Quantify your investment contributions:
Determine how much money you need to save or invest regularly to reach each investment goal within your set timeframe. Use financial calculators or investment planning tools to estimate the required contribution amounts.

8. Your investments need to align with your goals:
Choose investment vehicles and asset classes that align with your investment goals, timeframe, and risk tolerance. Consider diversifying your portfolio across stocks, bonds, cash equivalents, and alternative investments to manage risk and, in turn, maximise your returns.

9. Monitor investment progress and adjust as needed:
it is important to monitor your investment portfolio's performance regularly to track your progress toward each investment goal. Review and adjust your investment strategy as needed to stay on track with your goals, accommodate changing financial circumstances, and respond to changes in market conditions.

Building a diversified investment portfolio

Building a diversified investment portfolio is crucial for managing risk and maximising potential returns over the long term. Diversification involves spreading your investments across different asset classes, industries, geographic regions, and investment vehicles to reduce the impact of market volatility and mitigate specific risks. The steps below will guide you to successfully building a diversified investment portfolio:

1. Understand your risk tolerance:
Even though we have discussed risk tolerance in-depth, we need to reiterate how important it is to assess your risk tolerance and investment objectives to determine your comfort level with investment risk. Factors such as your investment goals, time horizon, financial situation, and willingness to tolerate fluctuations in portfolio value all need to be considered.

2. Define your asset allocation strategy:
Develop an asset allocation strategy that aligns with your risk tolerance, investment goals, and timeframe. Asset allocation involves determining the percentage of your portfolio allocated to different asset classes, such as stocks, bonds, cash equivalents, and alternative investments.

3. Allocate your assets across multiple asset classes:
Distribute your investment capital across different asset classes to build a diversified portfolio. Consider the risk-return characteristics of each asset class and how they complement each other within your overall investment strategy.

- **Stocks:** Equities offer long-term growth potential but come with higher volatility and risk. Consider diversifying across different sectors, market capitalisations, and geographic regions.
- **Bonds:** Fixed-income securities provide income and capital preservation but with lower risk and return potential compared to stocks. Diversify across different bond types, maturities, and credit qualities.
- **Cash Equivalents:** Cash equivalents, such as money market funds and Treasury bills, provide liquidity and stability but offer minimal returns. Allocate a portion of your portfolio to cash equivalents for short-term needs and liquidity.
- **Alternative Investments:** Consider incorporating alternative investments, such as real estate, commodities, or hedge funds, to further diversify your portfolio and potentially reduce overall portfolio risk.

4. Consider geographic diversification:
Spread your investments across different geographic regions and economies to reduce exposure to country-specific risks and capitalise on global growth opportunities. Consider investing in both domestic and international markets to diversify your portfolio's geographic exposure.

5. Diversify within asset classes:
Diversify within each asset class by investing in a broad range of securities or investment vehicles. For example:
- **Stocks:** Invest in individual stocks, mutual funds, exchange-traded funds (ETFs), or index funds across various sectors and industries.
- **Bonds:** Diversify across government bonds, corporate bonds, municipal bonds, and international bonds to mitigate credit and interest rate risk.
- **Real Estate:** Consider investing in real estate investment trusts (REITs) or real estate crowdfunding platforms to gain exposure to the real estate market without direct property ownership.

6. Rebalance regularly:
Periodically review and rebalance your investment portfolio to maintain your target asset allocation and risk profile. Rebalancing involves selling overperforming assets and reallocating funds to underperforming assets to bring your portfolio back in line with your desired asset allocation.

7. Monitor and adjust your investment portfolios as needed:
Various factors, your portfolio's performance, market conditions, and changes in your financial situation, need to be monitored regularly and adjusted to your investment strategy as needed to stay on track with your goals, accommodate changing market conditions, and respond to life events or financial milestones.

Building a diversified investment portfolio requires careful planning, ongoing monitoring, and disciplined execution. Always consider seeking guidance from a qualified financial advisor before embarking on any investment opportunities. They will help you develop a customised investment plan tailored to your individual goals, risk tolerance, and timeframe.

Chapter 6:
Retirement Planning

The importance of retirement planning

Retirement planning is another crucial aspect of your financial management that involves setting goals, saving, and investing to ensure financial security and well-being during your retirement years. Sadly this is one of the most overlooked components when it comes to successful financial planning.

It is always best to start planning early. The earlier you start with your retirement investments, the more comfortable you will be, financially, once you retire. Some companies also offer company benefits such as employer-sponsored retirement plans, that make successful retirement planning easier on you as an individual.

Unfortunately, as with so many people, this realisation comes much too late in life, leaving them with a limited investment horizon and subsequently falling short of their financial goals. The detailed explanation below highlights the importance of retirement planning:

1. Financial independence: Retirement planning allows individuals to achieve financial independence and maintain their desired lifestyle after they stop working. By saving and investing for retirement, individuals can build a nest egg that generates income to cover living expenses, healthcare costs, and leisure activities during retirement.

2. Longevity risk: With advancements in healthcare and improvements in living standards, people are living longer than ever before. Retirement planning helps individuals prepare for a potentially lengthy retirement period and ensures that they have enough savings to support themselves throughout their golden years.

3. **Maintaining your lifestyle:** Retirement planning enables individuals to maintain their current lifestyle or even upgrade it during retirement. By estimating future expenses and income needs, individuals can develop a savings and investment strategy that aligns with their retirement goals and aspirations.

4. **Inflation protection:** The cost of living tends to increase over time due to inflation, eroding the purchasing power of money. Retirement planning helps individuals stay ahead of rising costs by building a retirement fund that keeps pace with inflation and maintains their standard of living throughout retirement.

5. **Reduces family dependency:** Retirement planning reduces individuals' dependency on Social Security benefits and traditional pension plans, which may not provide sufficient income to support their retirement needs. By supplementing these sources of income with personal savings, investments, and retirement accounts, individuals can bridge any income gaps and achieve financial security in retirement.

6. **Healthcare expenses:** Healthcare costs tend to rise as individuals age, making healthcare expenses a significant consideration in retirement planning. By saving and investing for retirement, individuals can build a healthcare fund to cover medical expenses, long-term care, and other healthcare needs during retirement.

7. **Legacy planning:** Retirement planning allows individuals to leave a legacy for their loved ones or support charitable causes that are important to them. By carefully managing their finances and estate planning, individuals can ensure that their assets are distributed according to their wishes and leave a lasting impact for future generations.

8. **Early retirement goals:** No one wishes to work well into their retirement years. This is why it is important to note that proper retirement planning can also support early retirement goals. By helping individuals accumulate enough savings, they can retire ahead of schedule if desired.

By setting clear retirement goals and developing a disciplined savings and investment strategy, individuals can work towards achieving financial independence and retiring on their terms.

In summary, retirement planning is essential for achieving financial security, maintaining a lifestyle, and enjoying a fulfilling retirement. It provides individuals with the peace of mind that comes from knowing they have taken steps to secure their financial future and can enjoy their golden years without financial worries.

Types of retirement accounts

There are several types of retirement accounts available, each offering different tax advantages, contribution limits, and withdrawal rules. Here are the most common types of retirement accounts to look into:

1. 401(k) Plans:
These plans are employer-sponsored retirement plans offered by private companies and some non-profit organizations.
- Employees contribute a portion of their pre-tax income, which is often matched by the employer.
- Contributions grow tax-deferred until withdrawal, and withdrawals are taxed as ordinary income in retirement.
- Contribution limits are set annually by the IRS and may include catch-up contributions for individuals aged 50 and older.

2. Traditional individual retirement accounts (IRAs):
IRAs are available to individuals who have earned income and do not have access to an employer-sponsored retirement plan.
- Contributions may be tax deductible, depending on income and participation in an employer plan.
- Earnings grow tax-deferred until withdrawal, and withdrawals are taxed as ordinary income in retirement.
- Contribution limits are set annually by the IRS and may include catch-up contributions for individuals aged 50 and older.

3. Roth individual retirement accounts (IRAs):

Roth IRAs are funded with after-tax contributions, meaning contributions are not tax-deductible.

- Earnings grow tax-free, and qualified withdrawals in retirement are tax-free.
- Roth IRAs have income limits that determine eligibility for contributions.
- Contributions can be withdrawn penalty-free at any time, but earnings may be subject to taxes and penalties if withdrawn before age 59½.

4. Roth 401(k) plans:

Similar to Roth IRAs, Roth 401(k) plans are offered by employers and allow employees to make after-tax contributions.

- Contributions are not tax-deductible, but earnings grow tax-free, and qualified withdrawals in retirement are tax-free.
- Unlike Roth IRAs, Roth 401(k) plans do not have income limits, allowing high-income earners to contribute.
- Contributions can be made through payroll deductions, and employers may offer matching contributions.

5. Simplified employee pension (SEP) IRAs:

SEP IRAs are retirement plans available to self-employed individuals and small business owners, including sole proprietors and partnerships.

- Employers can contribute up to 25% of their net self-employment income or a maximum dollar amount set by the IRS, whichever is less.
- Contributions are tax-deductible, and earnings grow tax-deferred until withdrawal, taxed as ordinary income in retirement.

6. Solo 401(k) plans (individual 401(k) plans):

Solo 401(k) plans are retirement plans available to self-employed individuals with no employees other than a spouse.

- Similar to traditional 401(k) plans, contributions are made with pre-tax income, and earnings grow tax-deferred until withdrawal.
- Contribution limits are higher than traditional IRAs and may include catch-up contributions for individuals aged 50 and older.

- Solo 401(k) plans also offer the option for Roth contributions, allowing after-tax contributions with tax-free withdrawals in retirement.

7. Defined benefit plans (pensions):
Defined benefit plans are employer-sponsored retirement plans that provide retirees with a predetermined monthly benefit based on salary and years of service.
- Contributions are made by the employer, and investment decisions are managed by the plan sponsor.
- Retirement benefits are typically based on a formula that considers factors such as salary, years of service, and age at retirement.

These are the main types of retirement accounts available, each offering different features and benefits to help individuals save and invest for retirement. It's essential to understand the characteristics of each type of account and choose the ones that best align with your retirement goals, financial situation, and tax considerations. Consulting with a financial advisor can help you make informed decisions about retirement planning and investment strategies tailored to your specific needs.

Calculating your retirement savings needs

Calculating your retirement savings needs involves estimating how much money you'll need to cover living expenses and other financial obligations during your retirement years. Below is a guide to help you determine your retirement savings goal:

1. Estimate your retirement expenses:
Estimate all your retirement expenses, including essential living expenses such as housing, utilities, food, transportation, healthcare, and taxes. Consider your current spending habits and lifestyle preferences, as well as any changes you anticipate in retirement.

2. Remember to consider inflation:

Factor in the impact of inflation on your retirement expenses. Inflation erodes the purchasing power of money over time, so you'll need to account for the rising cost of living when estimating future expenses. Use a conservative inflation rate of around 2-3% per year for your calculations.

3. Determine your retirement age:

Decide at what age you plan to retire. Your retirement age will influence the length of your retirement period and the number of years your retirement savings will need to last. Consider factors such as Social Security eligibility, healthcare costs, and personal preferences when choosing your retirement age.

4. Calculate your retirement income needs:

Work out how much annual income you'll need during retirement to cover your expenses. A common rule of thumb is the "replacement ratio," which suggests replacing 70-80% of your pre-retirement income in retirement. Adjust this ratio based on your circumstances, retirement goals, and lifestyle expectations.

5. Factor in social security and other income sources:

It is important to take into account any other sources of retirement income, such as Social Security benefits, pensions, annuities, rental income, or part-time work. Determine how much income you expect to receive from these sources and subtract it from your total retirement income needs.

6. Calculate your retirement savings goal:

Once you have estimated your annual retirement income needs, multiply this amount by the number of years you expect to be retired to calculate your total retirement savings goal. For example, if your estimated annual retirement expenses are $50,000, and you plan to retire at age 65 and live until age 90, you would need to save $50,000 x 25 years = $1,250,000.

7. Make use of retirement planning tools:
Consider using retirement planning calculators or online tools to help you estimate your retirement savings needs more accurately. These tools can take into account various factors such as inflation, investment returns, and longevity risk to provide a more comprehensive analysis of your retirement readiness.

8. Remember to review and adjust regularly:
Periodically review and adjust your retirement savings goal as your financial situation, lifestyle preferences, and retirement expectations change over time. Revisit your retirement plan annually or after significant life events to ensure you're on track to achieve your retirement goals.

By following these steps and carefully estimating your retirement expenses, income needs, and savings goals, you can develop a personalized retirement plan that aligns with your financial objectives and provides peace of mind for your future retirement years. If you're unsure about your retirement savings needs or investment strategy, consider consulting with a financial advisor for professional guidance and advice tailored to your circumstances.

Strategies to maximise your retirement savings

Your retirement savings is essential for ensuring financial security and peace of mind during your golden years. Here are some expert strategies to help you boost your retirement savings:

1. Start early:
It is absolutely crucial to keep in mind that time is one of your most valuable assets when it comes to saving for retirement. The earlier you start saving, the more time your investments have to grow through compound interest. Even small contributions made early on can have a significant impact on your retirement nest egg.

2. Take advantage of employer-sponsored retirement plans:
Contribute to employer-sponsored retirement plans such as 401(k), 403(b), or Thrift Savings Plan (TSP) if available.

These plans often offer tax advantages like pre-tax contributions, employer matching contributions, and tax-deferred growth. Aim to contribute enough to maximise any employer matching contributions, as this is essentially free money.

3. Contribute to individual retirement accounts (IRAs):
Boost your contributions to traditional or Roth IRAs each year. These accounts offer tax advantages and allow your investments to grow tax-deferred or tax-free. Consider contributing the maximum allowed by law, and take advantage of catch-up contributions if you're age 50 or older.

4. Automate your savings:
Set up automatic contributions to your retirement accounts from your paycheck or bank account. Automating your savings ensures consistency and discipline, making it easier to stick to your retirement savings goals.

5. Reduce expenses and increase your savings rate:
Review your budget and identify areas where you can cut expenses to free up more money for retirement savings. Redirect any savings from reduced expenses toward your retirement accounts. Aim to gradually increase your savings rate over time as your financial situation improves.

6. Invest wisely:
Allocate your retirement savings across a diversified portfolio of assets based on your risk tolerance, time horizon, and investment goals. Consider low-cost index funds or exchange-traded funds (ETFs) to minimize fees and maximise long-term returns. Regularly review and rebalance your investment portfolio to ensure it remains aligned with your objectives.

7. Take advantage of tax breaks:
 - Maximise tax-advantaged retirement accounts and take advantage of tax breaks available for retirement savings.

Contribute the maximum allowed to employer-sponsored plans, traditional IRAs, or health savings accounts (HSAs) to reduce your taxable income and grow your savings more efficiently.

8. Delay retirement or work part-time:

Although not always ideal delaying retirement or working part-time during retirement is a good way to continue earning income and delay drawing down your retirement savings. Working longer allows you to contribute more to your retirement accounts and reduces the number of years your savings need to last, increasing financial security in retirement.

9. Educate yourself and seek professional advice:

Stay informed about retirement planning strategies, investment options, and tax implications. Educate yourself through books, online resources, and financial planning workshops. Consider seeking guidance from a qualified financial advisor who can provide personalized advice and help you navigate complex financial decisions.

By implementing these strategies and making retirement savings a priority, you can maximize your savings potential and build a secure financial foundation for your retirement years. Remember that every dollar saved today can have a significant impact on your future financial well-being, so start saving and investing for retirement as soon as possible.

Chapter 7:
Saving for Other Financial Goals

Saving for education

A significant financial goal for many families is saving for education. There are several strategies available to help you save and prepare for educational expenses. By following the steps below and implementing a disciplined savings plan, you can effectively prepare for education expenses, providing financial support for your child's educational journey.

1. Set clear goals:
Determine the type of education you are saving for (e.g., college, vocational school) and estimate the total cost, including tuition, fees, room and board, books, and other expenses. Set specific savings goals based on these estimates and the number of years until your child starts school.

2. Always start early:
Begin saving for education as early as possible to take advantage of compound interest and maximize your savings potential. The longer your money has to grow, the more you can accumulate over time.

3. Explore tax-advantaged accounts:
Consider using tax-advantaged savings accounts specifically designed for education, such as 529 plans or Coverdell Education Savings Accounts (ESAs). These accounts offer tax-free growth and tax-free withdrawals when used for qualified education expenses.

4. 529 College savings plans:
A 529 plan is a state-sponsored investment account that allows you to save for education expenses. Contributions are made with after-tax dollars, but earnings grow tax-free, and withdrawals are tax-free when used for qualified education expenses. Some states offer tax deductions or credits for contributions to 529 plans.

5. Coverdell education savings accounts (ESAs):

Coverdell ESAs are another tax-advantaged option for education savings. Contributions are made with after-tax dollars, but earnings grow tax-free, and withdrawals are tax-free when used for qualified education expenses. ESA contributions have annual contribution limits and income eligibility restrictions.

6. Uniform Gifts to Minors Act (UGMA) or Uniform Transfers to Minors Act (UTMA) Accounts:

UGMA and UTMA accounts allow parents, guardians, or relatives to save and invest on behalf of a minor child. While not specifically designed for education savings, these custodial accounts offer flexibility in how funds are used and can be used to fund education expenses.

7. Regular savings accounts:

You can also save for education expenses in a regular savings or investment account. While these accounts don't offer the same tax advantages as 529 plans or ESAs, they provide flexibility and accessibility for education savings.

8. Automate your contributions:

Set up automatic contributions to your education savings accounts to ensure consistent and disciplined savings over time. Automating your savings makes it easier to stay on track with your savings goals and eliminates the temptation to spend funds earmarked for education.

9. Monitor and adjust as needed:

Regularly review your education savings goals, contributions, and investment performance. Adjust your savings strategy as needed based on changes in your financial situation, educational goals, or investment preferences.

10. Explore financial aid and scholarships:

In addition to saving, explore opportunities for financial aid, scholarships, grants, and other forms of assistance to help cover education expenses.

- Chapter 7: Saving for Other Financial Goals -

Saving for your home

One of the biggest life goals most individuals strive to achieve is the ability to buy a home for themselves or their families one day. Saving for property is a significant financial goal that requires careful planning and disciplined saving. Here are some steps to help you save for a home purchase:

1. Determine your budget:
Assess your financial situation, including your income, expenses, debts, and savings. Determine how much you can realistically afford to spend on a home purchase, taking into account down payment, closing costs, monthly mortgage payments, property taxes, insurance, and maintenance expenses.

2. Set a savings goal:
Set a specific savings goal for your home purchase, including the amount you need for a down payment, closing costs, and other expenses. Aim to save at least 20% of the home's purchase price for a down payment to avoid private mortgage insurance (PMI) and qualify for better loan terms.

3. Set a budget and cut expenses:
Create a monthly budget to track your income and expenses. Identify areas where you can cut back on discretionary spending and redirect those savings toward your home fund. Consider reducing non-essential expenses such as dining out, entertainment, subscriptions, and impulse purchases.

4. Automate your savings:
Set up automatic transfers from your checking account to a dedicated savings account earmarked for your home purchase. Automating your savings ensures consistency and discipline, making it easier to reach your savings goals over time.

5. Look into down payment assistance programs:
Research down payment assistance programs offered by federal, state, and local government agencies, nonprofit organizations, and employers.

These programs may provide grants, loans, or other assistance to help eligible buyers with down payment and closing costs.

6. Open a high-yield savings account:
A high-yield savings account or money market account will offer a competitive interest rate on your savings. Look for accounts with no monthly fees and easy access to funds while still offering a higher interest rate than traditional savings accounts.

7. Consider tax-advantaged accounts:
Explore tax-advantaged accounts such as a Roth IRA or a first-time homebuyer's IRA to save for a home purchase. Contributions to Roth IRAs can be withdrawn penalty-free for a first-time home purchase, while contributions to traditional IRAs may qualify for tax deductions.

8. Invest wisely:
If your home purchase is several years away, consider investing a portion of your savings in a diversified portfolio of stocks, bonds, and other assets to potentially earn higher returns. However, be mindful of the risks associated with investing and choose investments based on your risk tolerance and time horizon.

9. Avoid any major purchases:
We recommend that you do not indulge in any significant purchases or take on additional debt while saving for a home, as it will only set you back financially, making it that much toucher to reach your savings goal. Delay major expenses such as a new car, expensive vacations, or large home renovations until after you've purchased your home to avoid depleting your savings or increasing your debt load.

10. Focus and flexibility is key:
Stay focused on your savings goal and remain disciplined in your saving habits. Be prepared to adjust your savings plan as needed based on changes in your financial situation, housing market conditions, and homebuying timeline.

Saving for travel or other major expenses

Most individuals dream of a comfortable life, owning nice things, and the freedom to travel the world, to name but a few. By following these steps and maintaining disciplined saving habits, you can effectively save for travel or other major expenses, turning your dreams into reality.

1. Set clear goals for yourself:
Determine the purpose and scope of your travel or major expenses. Identify specific destinations, experiences, or purchases you want to save for and estimate the total cost, including transportation, accommodation, activities, and any other associated expenses.

2. Create a budget:
Develop a budget to track your income and expenses. Review your current spending habits and identify areas where you can cut back or reallocate funds towards your savings goal. Consider reducing discretionary expenses such as dining out, entertainment, shopping, and non-essential purchases.

3. Start a savings plan:
Set a realistic savings target and timeline for reaching your goal. Determine how much you need to save each month to achieve your target amount within your desired timeframe. Break down your savings goal into smaller, manageable milestones to track your progress along the way.

4. Automate your savings:
Set up automatic transfers from your checking account to a dedicated savings account earmarked for your travel or major expenses. Automating your savings ensures consistency and discipline, making it easier to stay on track with your savings goals.

5. Open a high-yield savings account:
Open a separate high-yield savings account or money market account specifically for your travel or major expense savings. Look for accounts that offer competitive interest rates and no monthly fees, allowing your savings to grow faster over time.

6. Cut expenses and boost your income:

Look for opportunities to cut expenses and increase your income to boost your savings rate. Consider reducing non-essential spending, negotiating bills or subscriptions, or taking on additional work or side gigs to generate extra income to put towards your savings goal.

7. Use windfalls wisely:

Allocate unexpected windfalls such as tax refunds, bonuses, or cash gifts towards your travel or major expense savings. Rather than spending windfalls impulsively, use them to accelerate your progress towards your savings goal and achieve your objective sooner.

8. Prioritise your spending:

Your spending should align with your savings goals and values. Evaluate each purchase based on its importance and contribution to your overall financial objectives. Delay or forgo non-essential purchases to free up more funds for your savings goal.

9. Research cost-saving strategies:

Explore cost-saving strategies to make your travel or major expenses more affordable. Look for discounts, deals, and special offers on transportation, accommodation, activities, and other expenses. Consider traveling during off-peak seasons or using rewards points and loyalty programs to reduce costs.

10. Stay motivated and flexible:

Celebrating milestones and progress along the way staying focused and motivated motivation can also assist in helping you achieve your savings goals. Be prepared to adjust your savings plan as needed based on changes in your financial situation, timeline, or priorities. Stay flexible and resilient in the face of unexpected challenges or setbacks.

Chapter 8:
Protecting Your Financial Future

The importance of insurance

Because we can't predict what might happen in the future, insurance has always, and will always play a crucial role in providing financial protection and peace of mind for individuals, families, businesses, and communities alike. Below are several reasons highlighting the importance of insurance:

1. Risk management:
Insurance helps individuals and businesses manage various risks and uncertainties by transferring the financial burden of unexpected events to an insurance company. It protects against potential losses due to accidents, illnesses, natural disasters, theft, liability claims, and other unforeseen circumstances.

2. Financial protection:
Insurance provides financial protection by covering the costs associated with repairing or replacing damaged property, paying medical bills, compensating for lost income, and settling legal claims. It helps individuals and families avoid financial hardship and maintain their standard of living in times of crisis.

3. Asset Protection:
Insurance safeguards valuable assets such as homes, vehicles, businesses, and personal belongings against loss or damage. It allows individuals and businesses to protect their investments and assets from unexpected events that could result in significant financial loss.

4. Healthcare coverage:
Health insurance helps individuals and families access essential medical services, treatments, and medications without incurring exorbitant out-of-pocket expenses. It covers medical costs for preventive care, doctor visits, hospitalization, surgeries, prescription drugs, and other healthcare needs, promoting overall health and well-being.

5. Liability protection:
Liability insurance protects individuals and businesses from legal claims and lawsuits alleging negligence, injury, property damage, or financial loss. It covers legal defense costs, court judgments, and settlement payments, shielding policyholders from potentially ruinous financial liability.

6. Business continuity:
Insurance is essential for businesses to maintain continuity of operations and recover from unexpected setbacks. Business insurance policies, such as property insurance, liability insurance, business interruption insurance, and key person insurance, help protect against financial losses stemming from property damage, lawsuits, disruptions, and other risks.

7. Compliance and legal requirements:
Insurance coverage is often required by law or regulatory authorities for individuals, businesses, and professionals to operate legally and meet specific obligations. Examples include auto insurance, homeowners insurance, workers' compensation insurance, and professional liability insurance.

8. Peace of mind:
Perhaps most importantly, insurance provides peace of mind and security for individuals, families, and businesses, knowing that they are protected against unforeseen risks and financial losses. It allows policyholders to focus on their personal and professional lives without constantly worrying about potential disasters or emergencies.

In a nutshell, insurance is a fundamental component of financial planning and risk management, offering vital protection, security, and peace of mind for individuals, families, businesses, and society as a whole. It helps mitigate the financial consequences of unexpected events, allowing individuals and organizations to navigate life's uncertainties with confidence and resilience.

Estate planning basics

Estate planning is the process of preparing for the distribution of your assets and wealth after your death or incapacitation. It involves making decisions about how your assets will be managed, who will inherit them, and who will make financial and medical decisions on your behalf if you become unable to do so. Here are the basics when it comes to estate planning:

1. Will: A will is a legal document that outlines how you want your assets to be distributed after your death. It allows you to specify beneficiaries for your property, designate guardians for minor children, and appoint an executor to oversee the distribution of your assets.

2. Trusts: A trust is a legal arrangement that allows a third party, known as the trustee, to hold assets on behalf of beneficiaries. Trusts can help you avoid probate, minimise estate taxes, and provide ongoing management of assets for beneficiaries who are minors or have special needs.

3. Power of attorney: A power of attorney is a legal document that authorises someone to act on your behalf in financial or legal matters if you become incapacitated. There are different types of powers of attorney, including general, limited, and durable powers of attorney, each with specific powers and limitations.

4. Healthcare directive: A healthcare directive, also known as a living will or advance directive, allows you to specify your wishes for medical treatment if you become unable to communicate them yourself. It may include instructions regarding life-sustaining treatments, organ donation, and end-of-life care preferences.

5. Beneficiary designations: Many assets, such as retirement accounts, life insurance policies, and bank accounts, allow you to designate beneficiaries to receive the assets upon your death. Review and update beneficiary designations regularly to ensure they reflect your current wishes and avoid unintended consequences.

6. Estate tax planning: Estate tax planning involves strategies to minimise estate taxes and maximise the amount of wealth transferred to your heirs. This may include gifting assets during your lifetime, establishing trusts, and taking advantage of estate tax exemptions and deductions.

7. Guardianship designations: If you have minor children, estate planning allows you to designate guardians who will care for them in the event of your death or incapacity. Choose guardians carefully and discuss your wishes with them to ensure they are willing and able to fulfill the role.

8. Review and update regularly: Estate planning is not a one-time event but a process that should be reviewed and updated regularly to reflect changes in your life circumstances, family dynamics, and financial situation. Life events such as marriage, divorce, birth, death, or significant changes in assets or income should trigger a review of your estate plan.

9. Consult with professionals: Estate planning can be complex, and it's essential to seek guidance from legal, financial, and tax professionals to ensure your plan is comprehensive, legally valid, and tax-efficient. An experienced estate planning attorney can help you navigate the process and create a plan that meets your specific needs and objectives.

10. Communicate your wishes: Finally, communicate your estate plan and wishes with your loved ones to ensure they understand your intentions and can support the implementation of your plan. Discussing sensitive topics such as end-of-life care, inheritance, and family dynamics openly and honestly can help prevent misunderstandings and conflicts down the road.

By addressing these key aspects of estate planning, you can protect your assets, provide for your loved ones, and ensure your wishes are carried out according to your wishes, even after you're no longer able to make decisions yourself.

Identity theft protection

Identity theft protection is a crucial component of personal financial security in today's digital age. It is important that you fully understand the basics of identity theft protection:

1. Understanding identity theft:
Identity theft occurs when someone steals your personal information, such as your Social Security number, driver's license number, financial account numbers, or other sensitive data, to commit fraud or other crimes in your name. This can include unauthorized charges on your credit cards, opening new accounts in your name, filing fraudulent tax returns, or even accessing your medical records.

2. Monitor your credit reports:
Regularly monitor your credit reports from the three major credit bureaus (Equifax, Experian, and TransUnion) to check for any unauthorized activity or suspicious accounts. You are entitled to one free credit report from each bureau every 12 months through AnnualCreditReport.com.

3. Freezing your credit:
Consider placing a freeze on your credit reports to prevent identity thieves from opening new accounts in your name. A credit freeze restricts access to your credit reports, making it more difficult for fraudsters to obtain credit using your information. You can freeze and unfreeze your credit reports as needed, typically for free.

4. Using fraud alerts:
Place fraud alerts on your credit reports to alert creditors to verify your identity before extending credit in your name. Initial fraud alerts last for one year and can be renewed, while extended fraud alerts last for seven years. Creditors are required to take additional steps to verify your identity when a fraud alert is present.

5. Securing personal information:
Safeguard your personal information and sensitive documents to prevent identity theft.

Shred documents containing personal information before disposing of them, use strong, unique passwords for online accounts, and avoid sharing sensitive information on public Wi-Fi networks or unsecured websites.

6. Being cautious online:
Be cautious when sharing personal information online and avoid clicking on suspicious links or downloading attachments from unknown sources. Phishing scams, where fraudsters impersonate legitimate organizations to trick individuals into revealing personal information, are common methods used by identity thieves.

7. Using identity theft protection services:
Consider enrolling in identity theft protection services offered by reputable companies. These services monitor your credit reports, scan the dark web for signs of your personal information being traded or sold, and provide assistance and support in the event of identity theft.

8. Reporting identity theft:
If you believe you are a victim of identity theft, act quickly to minimise the damage. Contact the companies or financial institutions involved, place fraud alerts on your credit reports, file a report with the Federal Trade Commission (FTC) at IdentityTheft.gov, and report the crime to your local law enforcement agency.

By understanding the basics of identity theft protection and taking proactive measures to safeguard your personal information, you can reduce the risk of becoming a victim of identity theft and protect your financial well-being.

Chapter 9:
Increasing Income

Negotiating a salary raise

Negotiating a salary raise can be a nerve-wrecking but essential process for advancing your career and improving your financial well-being. Here are some steps to help you negotiate a salary raise effectively:

1. Research and preparation:
Research industry standards and salary benchmarks for your position, skills, experience level, and geographic location. Use online resources, salary surveys, and professional networks to gather data on typical salary ranges and compensation packages.

2. Document your achievements:
Compile a list of your accomplishments, contributions, and value-added initiatives since your last salary review or performance evaluation. Highlight specific examples of how you have exceeded expectations, achieved significant results, or contributed to the success of your team or organization.

3. Know your worth:
Determine your desired salary range based on your research and assessment of your skills, experience, and market value. Be prepared to justify your salary request with concrete evidence of your qualifications, achievements, and contributions.

4. Choose the right timing:
Schedule a meeting with your manager or supervisor to discuss your salary raise request at an appropriate time. Avoid bringing up the topic during busy or stressful periods, such as right before a major project deadline or performance review cycle.

5. Practice effective communication:
Approach the salary negotiation conversation with confidence, professionalism, and assertiveness.

Clearly articulate your reasons for requesting a salary raise, emphasizing your contributions, value, and commitment to the organization.

6. Quantify your contributions:
Use quantifiable metrics, such as revenue generated, cost savings achieved, projects completed ahead of schedule, or performance improvements, to demonstrate the tangible impact of your work on the organization's bottom line.

7. Be flexible and open-minded:
Be prepared to negotiate and compromise if necessary. Consider alternative forms of compensation or benefits, such as additional vacation days, professional development opportunities, flexible work arrangements, or performance-based bonuses.

8. Anticipate objections and counterarguments:
Potential objections or concerns from your employer, such as budget constraints or performance issues should always be anticipated. Prepare persuasive responses and counterarguments to address these objections and reinforce your case for a salary raise.

9. Stay professional and positive:
Maintain a professional and positive demeanor throughout the negotiation process, even if the initial response is not what you hoped for. Express gratitude for the opportunity to discuss your salary raise request and remain open to constructive feedback.

10. Follow-up in writing:
After the salary negotiation meeting, follow up with a concise summary of the discussion, including any agreed-upon action steps or next steps. Document any commitments or agreements made during the meeting to ensure clarity and accountability.

By following these steps and approaching the salary negotiation process strategically and professionally, you can increase your chances of successfully securing a salary raise that reflects your worth and contributions to the organization.

Chapter 10:
Maintaining Financial Well-Being

Reviewing and adjusting your financial goals

Reviewing and adjusting your financial goals is an important step in maintaining financial health and adapting to changing circumstances. Here are some steps to help you review and adjust your financial goals:

1. Assess your current financial situation:
Begin by evaluating your current financial status, including your income, expenses, savings, debts, investments, and overall financial health. Review your budget, bank statements, investment accounts, and credit reports to gain a clear understanding of your financial standing.

2. Reflect on your long-term objectives:
Consider your long-term financial goals and aspirations, such as retirement savings, homeownership, education funding, debt repayment, and wealth accumulation. Determine if your existing goals are still relevant and aligned with your values, priorities, and life stage.

3. Evaluate your progress towards your goals:
Review your progress toward achieving your financial goals. Assess whether you are on track to meet your targets, exceed them, or fall short. Identify any obstacles or challenges that may have impeded your progress and consider adjustments to overcome them.

4. Identify changes in circumstances:
Take into account any changes in your personal or financial circumstances that may impact your goals, such as changes in income, expenses, employment status, family situation, health, or economic conditions. Adjust your goals accordingly to accommodate these changes.

5. Set S.M.A.R.T. goals:
Ensure your financial goals are Specific, Measurable, Achievable, Relevant, and Time-bound (as previously discussed in-depth). Define clear objectives with quantifiable targets and deadlines to keep yourself accountable and motivated.

6. Prioritise your goals:
Prioritise your financial goals based on their importance, urgency, and feasibility. Focus on goals that are most critical to your financial well-being and align with your immediate needs and long-term objectives.

7. Revise your goals as needed:
Be flexible and willing to revise your financial goals as circumstances evolve. Be open to adjusting timelines, reallocating resources, or revising targets to better reflect your current situation and future aspirations.

8. Seek professional guidance:
Consider seeking advice from a financial advisor or planner to help you review and adjust your financial goals. A professional can provide personalised recommendations, insights, and strategies tailored to your unique circumstances and objectives.

9. Monitor and track your progress:
Regularly monitor and track your progress toward your revised financial goals. Review your goals periodically to assess performance, make necessary adjustments, and celebrate achievements along the way.

By regularly reviewing and adjusting your financial goals, you can ensure that your financial plan remains relevant, realistic, and effective in helping you achieve financial success and security over time.

Monitoring and reassessing finances

By regularly monitoring and reassessing your finances, you can maintain financial stability, make informed decisions, and work towards achieving your long-term financial goals. This crucial aspect of financial management allows you to stay on track toward your goals and adapt to changing circumstances. Here is how you effectively monitor and reassess your finances:

1. Regularly review your budget:
Set aside time each month to review your income and expenses. Compare your actual spending to your budgeted amounts and identify any discrepancies or areas where you may be overspending. Adjust your budget as needed to reflect changes in income, expenses, or financial goals.

2. Track your cash flow:
Keep track of your cash flow by monitoring your inflows and outflows of money. Track all sources of income and categorise your expenses to gain insights into your spending patterns. Use budgeting apps, spreadsheets, or financial software to streamline the process and gain a clear picture of your financial situation.

3. Monitor your debt:
Regularly monitor your debt levels, including credit card balances, loans, and other liabilities. Track your progress in paying down debt and aim to reduce high-interest debt first. Consider refinancing or consolidating debt to lower interest rates and accelerate repayment.

4. Review your savings and investments:
Monitor the performance of your savings and investment accounts regularly. Review the allocation of your investments to ensure they align with your risk tolerance, timeframe, and financial goals. Rebalance your portfolio periodically to maintain diversification and optimise returns.

5. Check your credit report regularly:

Obtain a free copy of your credit report from each of the three major credit bureaus (Equifax, Experian, and TransUnion) at least once a year. Review your credit report for inaccuracies, errors, or signs of identity theft. Dispute any discrepancies and take steps to improve your credit score if necessary.

6. Assess your financial goals:

Reassess your financial goals regularly to ensure they remain relevant, achievable, and aligned with your values and priorities. Consider any changes in your life circumstances, such as career advancements, family changes, or economic factors, that may impact your goals.

7. Evaluate how prepared you are for financial emergencies:

Assess the adequacy of your emergency fund to cover unexpected expenses or income disruptions. Aim to maintain three to six months' worth of living expenses in a readily accessible savings account. Adjust the size of your emergency fund based on changes in your financial situation or risk factors.

8. Stay informed and educated:

Stay informed about personal finance topics, economic trends, and changes in tax laws or regulations that may impact your finances. Take advantage of educational resources, workshops, or seminars to expand your financial knowledge and make informed decisions.

9. Stay committed and flexible:

Remain committed to your financial goals and make adjustments as needed to stay on track. Be flexible and willing to adapt your plans in response to changing circumstances or unexpected events. Celebrate your progress and achievements along the way to stay motivated and focused on your financial journey.

Seek professional financial advice when needed

Seeking professional financial advice can be a smart investment in your financial future, providing you with the guidance, support, and expertise you need to achieve your goals and build a secure and prosperous financial future. Consider these key areas when seeking professional financial advice:

Expertise and knowledge
Financial advisors have specialised knowledge and expertise in various aspects of personal finance, including investments, retirement planning, tax strategies, insurance, and estate planning. They can provide valuable insights and recommendations based on their expertise and experience.

Objective and unbiased advice
A financial advisor can offer objective and unbiased advice tailored to your unique financial situation, goals, and risk tolerance. Unlike family members, friends, or colleagues who may have their own biases or interests, a professional advisor acts in your best interests and provides impartial recommendations.

Personalised financial planning
A financial advisor can help you develop a personalised financial plan tailored to your specific needs, goals, and circumstances. They can assess your current financial situation, identify your short-term and long-term objectives, and develop strategies to help you achieve them.

Investment management
Financial advisors can help you navigate the complexities of investing and develop an investment strategy aligned with your goals and risk tolerance. They can recommend appropriate investment options, asset allocations, and portfolio diversification strategies to optimise returns and manage risk.

Retirement planning

Planning for retirement is a complex and multifaceted process that requires careful consideration of various factors, including savings, investments, Social Security, pension benefits, healthcare costs, and longevity risk. A financial advisor can help you develop a comprehensive retirement plan to ensure you can retire comfortably and achieve your desired lifestyle in retirement.

Risk management and insurance

Financial advisors can assess your insurance needs and recommend appropriate risk management strategies to protect you and your family against unexpected events, such as disability, illness, premature death, or property damage. They can help you evaluate different insurance options, such as life insurance, disability insurance, health insurance, and long-term care insurance, and determine the right coverage levels for your needs.

Tax planning and optimisation

Tax planning is an integral part of financial planning that can help you minimise your tax liabilities and maximise your after-tax income and wealth. Financial advisors can develop tax-efficient strategies to optimise your tax situation, reduce tax burdens, and take advantage of available tax deductions, credits, and incentives.

Financial education and empowerment

Working with a financial advisor can provide you with valuable financial education and empower you to make informed decisions about your money. Advisors can help demystify complex financial concepts, clarify your options, and educate you about the pros and cons of different strategies, allowing you to take control of your financial future.

Peace of mind

Finally, working with a financial advisor can provide you with peace of mind knowing that you have a trusted partner and ally who is looking out for your best interests and helping you navigate the complexities of personal finance.

Conclusion

Go forth and prosper!

Your journey through this comprehensive guide to financial well-being has equipped us with a wealth of knowledge and actionable insights to navigate the complexities of personal finance. We've explored key principles, strategies, and best practices that are essential for achieving financial security, stability, and success.

Throughout our exploration, we've emphasized the importance of understanding your current financial situation, setting clear and achievable goals, and developing a plan to reach those goals. From budgeting and saving to investing and retirement planning, each aspect of personal finance plays a crucial role in shaping our financial future.

By now, you've learned how to create a realistic budget, track your expenses, and prioritize your spending to align with your values and goals. You've discovered the power of saving and investing wisely to build wealth over time and achieve financial independence. You've also gained insights into the importance of protecting your financial assets through insurance, estate planning, and risk management strategies.

But knowledge alone is not enough. To truly improve your financial well-being, you must take action. Now is the time to implement the strategies and principles outlined in this guide and make meaningful changes to your financial habits and behaviors. Whether it's paying off debt, increasing your savings rate, or diversifying your investment portfolio, every step you take brings you closer to your financial goals.

Don't be discouraged by setbacks or challenges along the way. Financial well-being is a journey, and like any journey, it requires patience, persistence, and resilience. Stay focused on your goals, stay disciplined in your approach, and stay committed to your financial plan..

- *Conclusion* -

Remember, the choices you make today will shape your financial future tomorrow. By taking control of your finances and making smart decisions now, you're laying the foundation for a more secure and prosperous future. So, embrace the opportunity to transform your financial life, and take the first step towards a brighter tomorrow.

As you embark on this journey, remember that you're not alone. Seek support from trusted advisors, friends, and family members who can offer guidance, encouragement, and accountability along the way. Together, we can all achieve financial well-being and build the lives we've always dreamed of.

Ultimately, the choice to improve your financial well-being rests in your hands. By taking proactive steps to manage your money wisely, you can build a brighter future for yourself and your loved ones, free from financial stress and uncertainty. So, seize the opportunity to transform your financial life today and embark on the path towards greater security, stability, and success. Your future self will thank you for it

"Financial peace isn't the acquisition of stuff. It's learning to live on less than you make, so you can give money back and have money to invest. You can't win until you do this."

- Dave Ramsey -